~ SOUTHAMPTON'S ~

LOST PUBS

~ SOUTHAMPTON'S ~
LOST PUBS

Dave Goddard & Jim Brown

First published 2014 by DB Publishing, an imprint of JMD Media Ltd, Nottingham, United Kingdom.

ISBN 9781780914510

Printed and bound by Copytech (UK) Limited, Peterborough

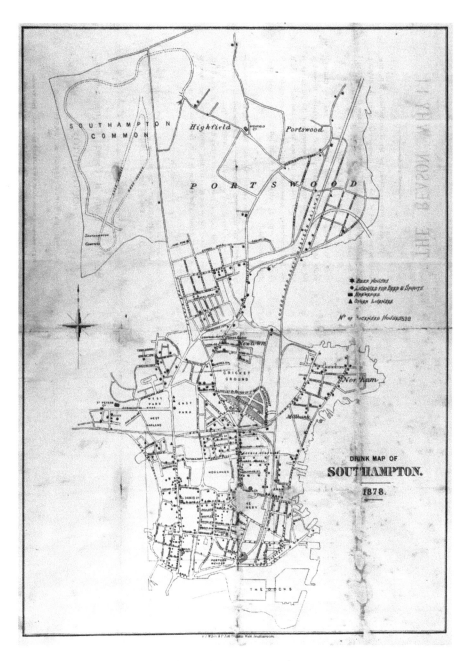

Courtesy of Southampton Archive Services

Introduction

Tribute must first be paid to Mrs Joyce Gallaher who gave permission for her late husband's photo collection to be used. Without the vast number of photos obtained by Tony Gallaher over several decades, this book would not be possible. Tony also obtained information relating to each public house, extracts of which have been freely used. Photos obtained from other sources have been suitably acknowledged.

Tony Gallaher's book *"Southampton's Inns and Taverns"* contains the names of nearly 1,000 Southampton public houses, (including the many name changes of individual premises) and he managed to obtain photos of a large percentage. Efforts have been made by the co-authors to obtain further photos, also to discover which ones are no longer pubs or have been demolished. It is therefore possible that the reader may know of other vanished public houses. This may be because either we do not possess a photo of the original premises, or are unaware of its demise. The loan of photos of now vanished public houses not shown in the book would be appreciated, for copying by co-author Dave Goddard (023 8073 7870).

It must also be stressed that modern photos cannot always be taken from exactly the same position as the original, also a different camera lens can give a different impression. Although every effort has been made to show the exact site, extensive area development can often mean that the precise location cannot be pin-pointed with 100% accuracy. Even so, the reader will nevertheless be aware of how the site of the original pub has changed, often beyond recognition.

The 1840's marked the town as a passenger port and with the coming of the railway the town prospered as never before. New hotels, inns, taverns and beer houses sprang up to cater for the increased number of residents, as well as workers engaged in constructing the docks, railways and buildings, followed by an ever-increasing number of dock workers, seamen and visitors. Many were just working men's pubs that could be found on almost every street corner in the lower town.

The 1878 "Drink Map of Southampton" showed each fully licensed premise by a red dot, each beer house by a red star, each brewery by a rectangle and all other licences by a triangle. In all there were 522 licenced premises in the much smaller town of that period, with a population of less than 80,000. This represented an average of one pub to every 153 residents.

The number of pubs began to decline when the Licensing Acts of 1904 and 1910 gave magistrates the power to refuse licences on the grounds that there were already too many in the area. Numbers decreased even further as a result of the World War Two blitz that destroyed the heart of the town, including many public houses. A further decline has come about in modern times as a result of the combination of increased and enhanced television in the home, coupled with the readily available cheaper alcohol in the local supermarkets. The more recent legislation prohibiting smoking inside premises has placed even more strain on those running a pub, this being the last straw for some who have reluctantly left the trade. This has forced many to become more of a restaurant than a pub. Co-author Jim Brown recalls being a teenager in the late 1940s when his parents ran the Dorset Ale House and Brewers Arms. His mother was in the forefront of not merely supplying crisps and nuts, as most pubs did, but also supplying sandwiches on demand.

It is hoped that the 350 photos in this book will bring back many memories for those who were 'regulars' in their local Southampton pub.

Dave Goddard & Jim Brown   September 2014

Southampton's Lost Pubs

This book is dedicated to the patrons of Southampton's public houses, so many of which have now disappeared. They were an asset to social drinkers, who shared their time with friends and family in the congenial atmosphere of a pub. Let us hope that many of the current public houses will remain untouched by the ever-spreading and relentless march of developers.

Aggie Grey's, 59 St Mary's Road

On the corner of St Mary's Road and Compton Walk, it was shown as a beer house on the 1878 Drink Map and had a beer licence prior to 1869. In August, 1916, the landlord, Philip Flint, was fined £5 10s for being drunk on the premises and for selling intoxicating liquor outside the permitted hours. A full licence was granted in March, 1960, when it was called *"The Halfway House"* (see over). Taken over by Strong's Romsey Brewery in the late 1920s, it became a Whitbread's house in 1969.

The premises are now a private club called *The Edge,* painted a distinctive purple colour and the rest of Compton Walk has virtually disappeared.

The corner of the premises are shown on the left, when under the name of *Halfway House,* and the large imposing Co-operative store at the bottom of Compton Walk dominated the area. The *Halfway House* closed when its licence lapsed on 5 April 1974. It reopened as the *Compton Arms* in October 1980 after £100,000 had been spent on complete modernisation and refurbishment.

The area has changed dramatically, with a massive block built on Charlotte Place in the left background and another residential block on the right, in front of the former Southern Gas administration building. The site of the former Co-operative block is now derelict.

Albany Hotel, 2/4 Winn Road

This free house, which stood on the corner of Winn Road and The Avenue, was known as the *Stafford House Hotel* from 1925 until December 1962, when it changed to the *Albany Hotel.* It was then modernised and greatly extended to include a bar – the *Venetian Bar* – that was open to non-residents.

The hotel closed for good in the Spring of 1989 and the building was demolished to make way for the above luxury apartments.

Albion Inn, 98 Bevois Valley Road

This pub dated back to the 1850s when brewer Tom Wolfreston was the landlord. It is shown as a beer house on the 1878 Drink Map. It was leased to Eldridge Pope's Dorchester Brewery in March 1914 and purchased by them in September 1927.

The former public house is now a popular student nightclub called *Sobar,* catering for the many university students of both the Southampton and Solent Universities.

Alfred Arms 82 Northam Road

This very small pub dates back to the 1860s when R.J. Andrews was the landlord. Shown as a beer house on the 1878 Drink Map, it was the property of Scrase's Star Brewery in the early part of the 20th Century. Strong's Romsey Brewery took over the premises in the 1920s and it became a Whitbread's house in 1969. Rumours are that it may reopen.

The *Alfred Arms* closed in 1982, with the adjacent former *Little Gems* now *The Desk Centre* and *Bygones* the internationally known *Cobwebs,* stocking much rare shipping memorabilia. Its proprietor, Peter Boyd-Smith, is an acknowledged authority on the *Titanic* disaster.

*(**Abrahams Collection**)*

Alma Inn, Almatade Road

When this pub, originally owned by Scrase's Star Brewery and later Strong's Romsey Brewery, opened in the 1860s it only had a six-day licence and did not obtain a full licence until 13 March 1951. It was taken over by the Whitbread Group in 1969 and closed for good on 4 August 1970.

Now a nicely maintained private house the owners have maintained the decorative bow windows and façade to keep the building in character.

Alma Inn 88/89 Alma Road

Like its Bitterne namesake, this pub, on the corner of Alma and Cambridge Roads, is named after the Crimean War battle of Alma in1854. Shown as a beer house on the 1878 Drink Map its address was then 35 Alma Road. The only recorded problem with the premises was in March 1916 when the landlord was fined £5 for allowing 'treating'. This wartime measure created the offence of buying a round of drinks, a somewhat strange offence.

After wartime damage it was repaired, modernised and rebuilt in the late 1940s. It was the property of Brickwoods' Brewery until 1971, when it was taken over by the Whitbread Group. It was subsequently replaced by a modern house.

Alton Ale House 8 West Street

This old pub, which stood roughly where Castle Way meets West Street, had a beer licence before 1869 and is shown as such on the 1878 Drink Map. In March 1917 landlord Graham Hayward was fined £2 for allowing 'treating'. Originally the property of Crowley's Alton Brewery, it was taken over by Watney, Coombe and Reid in 1947.

Its licence was placed in suspense on 8 May 1959 and it was demolished when the area was redeveloped. An office block now stands on the site.

Ampthill Hotel 72 Ampthill Road

Built in 1925, this pub, on the corner of Ampthill Road and Waterhouse Lane, Millbrook, was one of the last to be built for Scrase's Star Brewery before Strong's of Romsey took over. The name 'Scrase's' could still be seen in the etched-glass window when this photo was taken.

The pub became the property of the Whitbread Group in 1969 but was subsequently demolished and replaced by pleasant housing.

Anchor & Hope 125 Foundry Lane

Standing on the corner of Foundry Lane and Wolseley Road, this pub stands on the site of an older pub, the *Andover Inn* which dated back to the 1850s. It changed to *Anchor & Hope* in 1870 and was then in Wellington Road, the old name for Wolseley Road. Originally the property of Barlow's Victoria Brewery it was later owned by Brickwoods' Brewery but became a Whitbread's house in 1971.

Still retaining its former features, it is now a Co-operative Convenience Store.

Anchor & Hope 56 Threefield Lane

Standing on the corner of Threefield Lane and the remaining portion of Chandos Street, it was leased to Eldridge Pope's Dorchester Brewery in 1875 and is shown as a beer house on the 1878 Drink Map. However, it dates back to the 1840s when James Cave, a coach painter and brewer, was the landlord.

It had a major face-lift in 1988 and a further refurbishment in 1994, but was demolished in 2004 and replaced by a modern block of apartments.

The Anchor 76 East Street

This pub was known as the *Oriental Arms* in the early 1860s and the 1878 Drink Map shows a fully licensed house on the site.

By the 1880s it was known as the *Anchor Stores as* it was associated with the nearby Anchor Brewery. It became the property of Strong's Romsey Brewery in the 1920s, probably when the present building was erected.

It belonged to the Whitbread Group by 1969 and early in 1993 transformed into a Whitbread cask ale house with a bare uncomfortable interior and renamed the *Hogshead and Anchor.*

Closed by August 2014 the building now present a sorry site and is no doubt awaiting development into some form of residential accommodation.

(*Abrahams Collection*)

Angel Inn 412 Bitterne Road

An old coaching inn, dating back to the 1840s, when the landlord was William Pottinger. It was once owned by Cooper's Brewery but later became a Watney's house when it closed in 1972.

Demolished in August 1972 to make way for an extended Sainsbury's Supermarket.

Antelope Hotel 66 St Mary's Road

This old Cooper's Brewery premises stood on the corner of St Mary's Road and Bellevue Street and is shown as a fully licensed house on the 1878 Drink Map. It was closely associated with the Antelope Cricket Ground on the opposite side of St Mary's Road and it was in these premises that the *Hampshire County Cricket Club* was formed in 1863.

The *Antelope* closed in April 1931 and the site is now occupied by development on Charlotte Place and a modern road system.

Arrow Inn 33 Chapel Road

Standing on the corner of Chapel Road and Granville Street, it was known as the *Barge Tavern* in the 1840s but changed its name to *Arrow Inn* in honour of the yacht *Arrow* (based in a nearby Chapel boatyard) which won the America Cup in 1851.

Leased to Eldridge Pope's Dorchester Brewery on 6 June 1857, it closed on 23 October 1965 following a compulsory purchase order and was replaced by industrial buildings.

Bald Faced Stag 36 Edward Road

Standing on the corner of Edward and Kentish Roads, it dates back to the 1870s and was simply known as the *Stag Inn* in the 1880s, changing to its present name around 1890. In October 1916 the landlady, Olive Fleming, was fined £1 for selling drink outside permitted hours.

It was owned by the Winchester Brewery, later Marston's Brewery, and closed in 2011 to become residential accommodation.

Bassett Hotel 111 Burgess Road

Standing on the corner of Burgess and Butterfield Roads, the landlord in 1871 proudly boasted the name of George Washington Jones. In the early 1930s it was famous for its gardens and bear pit (with real bears), created by its landlord, Arthur Cornish-Trestrail.

Home of the *Concord Club*, renowned for its celebrity jazz concerts, it was refurbished at great cost in 1972, but by 2006 was replaced by the Sunrise Senior Living complex.

Bay Tree Inn 10 New Road

Dating back to the 1850s, it survived the World War Two blitz, although badly damaged by nearby bombing. It was demolished and replaced by the present structure in 1955, when it was owned by George Gale & Co's Horndean Brewery.

It has now been converted to private residential accommodation.

Beehive Inn 10 Millbrook Road

This was a beer house in the 1830s when George Evans was landlord and by 1934 it belonged to Brickwoods' Brewery. It was not granted a full licence until 8 March 1960 and became the property of the Whitbread Group in 1971.

Not far from Four Posts Hill, it was demolished in November 1977 and replaced by a modern office block.

Bell and Crown 40 Melbourne Street

On the corner of Melbourne and Standford Streets, it dated back to the early 1850s when Tom Bell, who also ran a carriage business, was landlord. It is shown as a fully licensed house on the 1878 Drink Map, when it was called the *British Queen*. .

The pub's licence was temporarily suspended in October 1947 and bought by the local authority under a compulsory purchase order 27 January, 1966, when it was demolished to make way for the above development.

Belvedere Arms 1 Belvidere Road

This was a private residence until September 1868 when it was leased by Welsh's Lion Brewery for 21 years at an annual rent of £20.00. Shown as a beer house on the 1878 Drink Map, it changed its name to *Belvidere Inn (note spelling)* around 1908. It was once known locally as the *Mud and Duck,* originating from one of the landlords keeping ducks on a muddy piece of land at the side of the pub. In September 1914 landlord Reg Needham was fined 5/- (25p) for assaulting a customer.

It closed in 1931 and the building used as an office by the nearby Phoenix Coal Company until demolished in the 1960s for development.

Bevois Castle Hotel 3 Bevois Street

Shown as a fully licenced house on the 1878 Drink Map, it dates back to the early 1840s when there was just Fanny Lock's brewery on the site. It changed name to *Bevois Street Tavern* until at least 1934, when it reverted back to *Bevois Castle Hotel*. It was owned by Gale's Horndean Brewery until bought by the local authority under a compulsory purchase order on 8 August 1964.

Close to Kingsland Square market and the Kingsland Tavern, the building was demolished shortly after 1964, but its licence was not surrendered until 4 October 1965.

Bevois Town Hotel 6 Middle Street

Dating back to the early 1860s, and standing on the corner of Middle and Liverpool Streets, it was shown as a fully licensed house on the 1878 Drink Map. It belonged to the Winchester Brewery prior to becoming a Marston's House.

Closed and boarded up in 2014, the building is awaiting occupants, presumed as a private residence.

Black Bull 85 St Andrew's Road

This stood on the corner of St Andrew's Road and Magdalene Terrace and had a beer licence from before 1869, when James Balls was the landlord. It belonged to Aldridge's Bedford Brewery but its licence was suspended on 28 October 1942 after it suffered severe bomb damage. It was then transferred to Brickwoods' Brewery in December 1942.

The site has since disappeared in the post-war development around the old Six Dials area.

Blacksmith's Arms 197 **Romsey Road**

Standing on the corner of Romsey and Winchester Roads, this pub dates back to the 1840s when John Webber was the landlord. It once belonged to Cooper's Brewery and in 1990 had the new name of *Ringside*, assumed to be because the landlord was a pugilist? It later became a Watney's house when sold to new owners early in 1993 and reverted to its original name.

Closed in 2013, the former pub has been redeveloped as a residential property with new houses along both sides.

Bridge Inn 28 Cracknore Road

This pub had a licence prior to 1869 and was owned by Scrase's Star Brewery. In its early days it was known as the _Railway Bridge Inn_ after the nearby footbridge over the London and Bournemouth railway line. Cracknore Road was then known as Lodge Road.

It was later owned by Strong's Romsey Brewery and then taken over in 1969 by the Whitbread Group. It closed 5 April 1974 and is now a private residence.

Bridge Tavern 70 Coxford Road

The original pub on this site dates back to the 1880s, when it was known as the *Coxford Bridge Tavern* because it stood by the road bridge over Tanner's Brook. In 1906 landlord William Savage was fined £1.00 for permitting drunkenness on the premises.

The building was erected for Mew Langton's Newport Brewery in the 1930s but now stand empty awaiting development.

Bridge Tavern 106/108 New Road

Standing on the corner of New Road and St Mary Street, it is believed that in the 1830s it was called the *Red Rover* after the stage coach that ran from Southampton to London. It was renamed *Bridge Tavern* in the 1850s and is shown as fully licensed on the 1878 Drink Map. It belonged to Forder's Hampton Court Brewery until July 1925 when it became the property of Brickwoods' Brewery but taken over by the Whitbread Group in 1971

It became an Art Gallery for a period but is now closed and offered To Let.

Britons in Union 6 Lower Canal Walk

It dates back to the 1850s when Jane Ward was the landlady. It was the property of Barlow's Victoria Brewery and became a Brickwoods' house in 1925.

It was demolished when the area was cleared of slums and redeveloped in the 1930s. Pleasant apartments are now on the site.

Builder's Arms 7 Union Street

It dates back to 1863 when it was leased to John Snook by the Bishop of Winchester. It was taken over by Crowley's Alton Brewery in 1902 and in 1909 landlord Mr Weeks was fined 10/- (50p) for selling drink to a drunken person. It became a Watney's house in 1947 but its licence was suspended 24 February 1956 and it was subsequently demolished.

Modern apartments now occupy the site.

The Bull's Eye Butts Road

Standing on the corner of Butts and Heathfield Roads, it opened in November 1955 and was the first new Watney's pub to be built in Southampton after World War Two. Its licence was transferred from the blitzed *Newcastle Inn* in East Street.

It closed for a while at the end of 1985 and re-opened after major refurbishment in February 1986. However, by 2014 it had become one of the Tesco Express convenience stores to be found throughout the country.

Burton Tavern 26 Orchard Lane

It had a licence from before 1869, when it was known as the *Burton Ale House*. Owned by Welsh's Hyde Abbey Brewery, Winchester, it later belonged to Cooper's Brewery and finally became a Watney's house.

Its licence was suspended 5 April 1957 when the area was extensively developed and the site became a block of pleasant apartments.

The Castle Witts Hill

Built for Cooper's Brewery in 1935 on the site of a former mock-Gothic Midanbury Castle, it was later owned by the Watney Group. Its licence originated from the *Forester's Arms* in West Street which had been surrendered. *The Castle* re-opened in December 1968 after a major refurbishment to become a 'Chef and Brewer' carvery.

Although it once again reverted to become an ordinary pub, it nevertheless subsequently closed down and has become a Tesco Express serving the area in a different way.

Chamberlayne Arms 79 North East Road

This dates back to the 1860s when William Pollard was the licensee. It was owned by Cooper's Brewery and later became the property of the Watney Group. It closed for a while at the end of 1988 for major alterations and reopened with a new modern image in January, 1989.

However, in the course of time its fortunes dwindled, it closed in 2013 and was later demolished. A *One Stop* convenience store is currently being constructed on the site.

Chichester Arms 26 Northam Road

This dates back to the early 1850s when Tom May was the landlord and the 1878 Drink Map shows it was then a beer house. Its first address was 12 Chichester Terrace, hence its name. Owned by Aldridge's Bedford Brewery, it was destroyed in a 1942 wartime air raid.

The site was derelict for many years, but an interesting bookshop has since been built in this fascinating part of Northam Road with its many antique shops.

Clarence Hotel 130 High Street

The original pub on this site was a nice four-storied pre-Victorian building with bow windows to the first and second floors. Dating back to the 1780s, when John Chidden was the landlord, it was known for years as *The Mitre,* changed to the *Bugle* around 1833 and finally the *Clarence Hotel* at the end of the 1830s, probably in honour of William IV who died in 1837. (He was formerly the Duke of Clarence).

Another name change came about in 1855 when it was called *Stephen's Hotel* but it later reverted back to *Clarence Hotel.*

The original old building survived World War Two, only to be demolished in the 950s to become a cane-furniture shop.

It is now an "authentic Indian restaurant" called the *Coriander Lounge.*

(*Abrahams Collection*)

Cliff Hotel Portsmouth Road

This pub, close to the start of the former hard for the old Floating Bridges, dates back to the 1830s when Isaac Jackman was the landlord and a coach service ran from the site. In the 1890s it was the headquarters for the St Mary's Football Club and in the 1950s home of the Southampton Rhythm Club.

Once a Cooper's pub and later a Watney's house, it closed for business towards the end of the 1980s and has now been converted into private apartments,

Clipper's Arms 17/18 James Street

Shown as a beer house on the 1878 Drink Map, it possessed a beer and wine licence prior to 1869. Shown as the *Shepherd's Arms* in the 1874 street directory, it was once the property of Crowley's Alton Brewery but later became a Watney's house.

It closed in 1965 and the entire area has since been extensively developed.

Crown & Sceptre 168 Burgess Road

It stands on the corner of Burgess and Broadlands Roads, on a site previously occupied by an old Scrace's beer house that dated back to the early 1870s when Richard Walters was the landlord. The above building was erected in 1930, not long after the original pub had been taken over by Strong's Romsey Brewery..

It became a Whitbread house in 1969 but was subsequently demolished and in early 2014 awaits further development.

Crown Hotel 73/75 Shirley High Street

Dating back to the early 1840s, when John James was the landlord, this Grade II listed building stands on the corner of Shirley High Street and Crown Street. It belonged to the Old Shirley Brewery in 1875 and was later taken over by Cooper's Brewery before becoming a Watney's house.

Later tied to the Morland Brewery of Abingdon, it was re-named *Tramways* for some time before becoming *The Crown*. It is currently closed and empty.

The Crown Hotel 14 High Street

Staff can be seen outside this old hotel, which dates back to Tudor times, and the photo on the left shows the front of the building, with its canopy, near the top of East Street with the front of All Saints Church seen in the background.

The 1878 Drink Map shows a fully licensed house on this site. Eldridge Pope's Dorchester Brewery obtained the lease in August 1938 but it was destroyed in an air raid on the night of 30 November, 1940.

At one period part of the large premises of Shepherd and Hedger (Maple), house furnishers, later a post office, it is currently a betting shop.

The Davis's 3 Terminus Terrace

Close to the Terminus Railway Station it is shown as a fully licensed house on the 1878 Drink Map. Owned by Robert Davis when it first opened in the 1850s it later was owned by Cooper's Brewery, later a Watney's house.

After a major face-lift it re-opened in December 1987, as a bar/nightclub called *Turpin's,* adding a Chinese/Thai restaurant in 1992, but later closed and is now private apartments.

Diamond Jubilee 65 Orchard Lane

On the corner of Orchard Lane and Mount Street, its name originated from Queen Victoria's diamond jubilee in 1897, but it was a beer house dating back to the early 1860s when George Dyett was the landlord.

Its licence was suspended on 13 March 1956 and it was demolished shortly after that to make way for extensive development in the area, mainly modern apartment blocks.

Dock Tavern 2 Endle Street

On the corner of Dock Street and Endle Street, the original premises were shown as fully licensed on the 1878 Drink Map. It was erected in the 1930s and belonged to Ashby's Eling Brewery, later owned by Strong's Romsey Brewery. It was acquired by the local authority under a compulsory purchase order on 29 June 1961, when it closed for good.

It survived the extensive development in the area and became the offices of the General Municipal, Boilermakers and Allied Trades Union, but later demolished and replaced by the above structure used by the B.T.C. Rowing Club

Dorset Ale House 12 Adelaide Road

Lived in when a teenager during the late 1940s by co-author Jim Brown, when his parents were the licensees, the 1878 Drink Map shows a beer house on this site, called the *Dorchester Arms*. Owned by Barlow's Victoria Brewery it later belonged to Brickwoods' Brewery and became a Whitbread's house in 1971. Although granted a full licence in 1959, it closed in 1974 and was later demolished.

Modern housing was subsequently developed over the site and adjacent properties.

Dorsetshire Arms 78 St Mary Street

Standing on the corner of St Mary and Johnson Streets, it dates back to the 1840s when Andrew Shutler was the landlord. Shown as a beer house on the 1878 Drink Map, it received a full licence in 1960. Owned by Aldridge's Bedford Brewery, then Brickwoods' Brewery, it became a Whitbread's house when it closed.

It later became a Clan Scotland club but now, in 2014, it is a general store under the appropriate name of "Kingsland".

Duchess of Wellington 2 Wolseley Road

Standing on the corner of Wolseley and Firgrove Roads and dating back to the 1860s, it was once known as the *Duke of Wellington,* changing to its present name in the late 1890s. In 1908 the landlord was fined £2.00 for failing to keep a record of his receipts for spirits. Owned by Scrase's Star Brewery it later belonged to Strong's Romsey Brewery and became part of the Whitbread Group in 1969.

It became the property of Wadworth's Devizes Brewery in early 1991 but it closed in 2011 to become a desirable private residence.

The Duke 58 Bernard Street

Edwin Ravenscroft owned the pub prior to 1869, when it was leased to Lovibond's Greenwich Brewery, then having the address of 14 Bernard Street. In the 1880s it was also an 'oyster house and dining room' and in April 1903 landlord Mr Morris was fined £1.00 for allowing drunkenness on the premises. It was destroyed in the war and the above temporary flat-roofed building erected on the site.

The licence was suspended on 7 November 1955 and the building demolished soon after. The Queensway dual carriageway now runs over the site.

Duke of York 40 York Street

Standing on the corner of York and Coburg Streets, it had a beer licence prior to 1869. Owned by Scrase's Star Brewery it was later taken over by Strong's Romsey Brewery. Its licence was suspended on 27 May 1958 and it was later demolished, although the licence wasn't finally surrendered until 4 October 1965.

A shopping parade now stands on the site and although many of the shops have closed residents still live above them.

Durham Tavern 42 Chapel Road

Located on the corner of Chapel Road and Marine Parade, it dates back to the late 1830s when it was known as the *Floating Bridge Tavern* and Charles Lawrence was the licensee. The name is thought to have changed in the 1870s. It was a Strong's Romsey Brewery pub for many years.

A Whitbread's house since 1969, its licence lapsed 21 October 1970 and the pub was demolished soon after.

The Eagle 150 Millbrook Road

It dates back to the 1860s when William Watts was the licensee. It was the property of Forder's Hampton Court Brewery and in March 1920 landlady Bessie Vere was fined £50.00 for selling overpriced whisky from an unmarked bottle! Owned by Brickwoods' Brewery in 1925 it was taken over by the Whitbread's Group in 1971.

It closed on 25 January 1981 and the Freemantle Business Centre was built on the site.

Edinburgh Hotel 1 St Mary's Road

Standing on the corner of St Mary's Road and St Andrews Road, it dates back to the early 1860s and the 1878 Drink Map shows it was fully licensed.

This shows the bomb damage at the top of St Mary's Street at the junction with the former Six Dials gyratory system, with the pub in the background.

The building was acquired under a compulsory purchase order after its licence was suspended on 20 February 1963 and it was demolished soon after when the entire area was redeveloped.

Elephant and Castle 112 Bursledon Road

The original pub dates back to the 1860s when it was nicknamed *The Old Black House* because of its corrugated iron walls and black tarpaulin roof. This building was erected in the 1930s, modernised in 1966 and refurbished again in the 1980s to become a 'Roast Inn' pub.

This photo was taken in September 2005 after it had closed and prior to the entire site being developed. The site of the former pub and its car park is now covered by 15 apartments and 19 terraced houses along Bursledon Road, those on the actual pub site shown below.

Engineer's Arms 98 Northam Road

Standing on the corner of Northam Road and Wilson Street, it dates back to the 1850s and is shown as a beer house on the 1878 Drink Map. Believed to be first called the *Victoria Arms,* J. Masters, the licensee in the 1870s, was an engine driver, probably why the name changed.

Welch's Lion Brewery took the pub over in July 1876 and later sold it to Scrase's Star Brewery for £500. It later belonged to Strong's Romsey Brewery but had been taken over by the Whitbread Group when it ceased trading on 31 January 1982. The premises are now occupied by a firm of dental technicians.

Equator Inn 36 Bedford Place

Although of poor quality, the photo nevertheless gives some idea of what the pub looked like. It dates back to 1845 when James Hall was the licensee. Welsh's Lion Brewery took out a seven year lease in 1872 and it later belonged to the nearby Aldridge's Bedford Brewery.

It was a Brickwoods' house when it ceased trading in the 1950s and became a fruit shop before its current City Photographic camera shop.

Exeter Hotel 23 Manchester Street

Standing on the corner of Manchester Street and Western Esplanade, opposite the old Lido, it dates back to the early 1850s and the 1878 Drink Map shows it was then fully licensed.

The entire length of Manchester Street was swept away during the construction of the ring road, the Marlands Shopping Mall and the multi-storey car park. The Marlands Shopping Mall, opened on 5 September 1991, was then the largest shopping centre in Southampton and the first significant shopping centre in the city.

Falcon Inn 24 Princes Street

Standing on the corner of Princes Street and Coburg Street since prior to 1869, the 1878 Drink Map shows it had a beer licence. It was once the property of Long's Southsea Brewery and later owned by Brickwoods' Brewery.

Its licence was placed in suspense on 24 October 1957 and the building was demolished soon after, to be replaced by an industrial site.

Fighting Cocks Redbridge Road

There was a *Swan Inn* near this site prior to 1851, a country pub that overlooked the old Millbrook Pond on the main road from Southampton. When the new Millbrook Roundabout was built in the early 1950s the *Swan Inn* found itself in a quiet cul-de-sac and when the increased traffic meant that a new flyover had to be built in the late 1960s, the *Swan Inn* was demolished to make way for it.

After the demise of *The Swan* the *Fighting Cocks* was built not far from *The Swan* site, at a cost of £40,000 and became the property of the Whitbread group in 1971. It eventually closed down and became a McDonald's.

Fireman's Arms 20 Chandos Street

On the corner of Chandos and Eldon Streets, it had a beer licence prior to 1868, when E. Sibley was the licensee. It was then known as the *Freemason's Arms* but changed to the *Fireman's Arms* in the 1880s.

It was owned by several brewers in turn, Welsh's Hyde Abbey, Cooper's and finally Watney's. Its licence finished on 20 June 1956 and it was demolished shortly afterwards, with modern council flats built on the site.

(Abrahams Collection)

Firs Inn 92 Pound Street

This dates back to the early 1870s when William Wyatt was the licensee. In 1806 it was a private house, owned by John Sennet, founder of the local Wesleyan Chapel. Once the property of Aldridge's Bedford Brewery, it later belonged to Brickwoods' Brewery.

When it closed down in 1974 it was part of the Whitbread Group, but was demolished and pleasant housing built on the site.

Floaters Hazel Road

Although not strictly speaking a public house, it is thought worthwhile to include the *Floaters* nightclub in the book because of its unusual and temporary nature. In 1978, shortly after the Itchen Bridge was completed in 1977, an enterprising individual decided to convert one of the disused floating bridges and turn it into a nightclub.

Floaters continued for a few years, but eventually closed as financially unviable.

The Gate 140 Burgess Road

Dating back to the 1840s, when William Egerton was the proprietor, it was an independent brewery for many years. Shown as the *Well Hung Gate* on the 1846 street map, it is listed as *Gate Hangs High* in the 1870 directory.

It became a Brickwoods' pub, part of the Whitbread Group in 1971 and then an independent brewery once again in the early 1980s when it was known as the *Gate Brewery*. Brewing then ceased and it was taken over by Eldridge Pope's Dorchester Brewery in early 1991. Despite efforts to save it by locals in 2010, it was later demolished and is now a vacant site.

The Gatehouse 14 Padwell Road

Formerly known as the *Royal Arms*, standing on the corner of Padwell and Oxford Roads, it dates back to the early 1830s when Charles Swanson was the landlord. Owned by Scrase's Star Brewery, it later belonged to Strong's Romsey Brewery before ending up as a Whitbread's house in 1969.

It narrowly escaped destruction, but was badly damaged in 1941 when a Heinkel II plane crashed onto the house opposite. It changed its name to *The Gatehouse* before closing in 2008 and is now being converted into flats.

Glasgow Hotel 75 Bernard Street

Standing on the corner of Bernard Street and Orchard Place, it was known as *Pullinger's Hotel* in the early 1840s and later as the *Clarendon* Hotel. It then boasted that the owner spoke fluent French and that it was a 'foreign wine establishment'. It was known as the *Glasgow Restaurant and Oyster Grotto* in 1925 but the original building was destroyed in the wartime blitz and replaced by a temporary flat-roofed shack.

The present building was erected for the Watney Group in 1958 as *The Glasgow* when the area was redeveloped. It changed to *Dixie's* in October 1990 but it subsequently closed and the premises are now occupied by Martin's Rubber Manufacturers.

The Globe 76 Bernard Street

Standing on the corner of Bernard Street and displaying the former entrance to Orchard Lane on the left, it is shown on the 1846 town map and as a fully licensed house on the 1878 Drink Map. It was owned by various breweries, Barlow's Victoria, Perkins Globe, Brickwoods' and finally Whitbread's. It closed in 1988 and was left derelict until 1991 when it was restored with plans to turn it into a trendy bar called *Harry Lime's*.

However, locals objected to an application for a music and dancing licence, so work ceased that year and it became a private residence.

The Globe Inn 55 Stratton Road

Standing on the corner of Stratton Road and Vaudrey Street, it was known as the *Globe Tavern* in the early 1880s and belonged to Barlow's Victoria Brewery. Stratton Road was then called Beavis Street. In March 1910 landlord Arthur Snelgrove was fined 10/- (50p) for selling beer to a drunken person.

Sometime after it became a Brickwoods' House its licence was suspended on 21 January 1966 and the building demolished shortly afterwards.

The Greyhound Inn Cossack Green

The 1878 Drink Map shows a beer house on this site and the above premises were erected on the site in the 1930s by the Strong's Romsey Brewery. Because it had been newly built it was spared when the area was cleared of slums during that period and it survived bombing when many of the surrounding buildings were destroyed in World War Two.

It stood alone among the debris for some years until it was surrounded by the low-rise flats during the 1950s. It closed for a year at the end of 1991, and although it re-opened in 1992 it was subsequently demolished and replaced by the above terraced housing.

Gurney Arms 27 Chantry Road

Standing on the corner of Chantry Road and Andersons Road, and owned by Barlow's Victoria Brewery, it had a beer licence prior to 1869 and was granted a full licence in March 1961. Its licence was suspended in July 1965 but before it was demolished it was used as part of a film set for the MGM film _Stranger in the House_ starring James Mason.

The entire area has now been extensively developed with modern apartments.

Hampton Park Hotel 77 High Road

Standing on the corner of High and Burgess Roads, it was opened in 1924 by Strong's Romsey Brewery. Its licence was refused in 1989 because of police having to deal with too many incidents of trouble with customers, but after it was restored the next month, trouble persisted and it closed and was boarded up. Closed for over a year it was completely refurbished and re-opened with the name of *Old Black Cat* in February 1991.

After becoming part of the Whitbread Group it became a free house belonging to the Devenish group of companies, but subsequently closed and is now a McDonald's.

The Haymarket 12/13 Hanover Buildings

The original building, on the corner of The Strand and complete with stables, was known as the *Yeoman Inn* in 1811 and it changed to *Haymarket Tavern* in 1865. In August 1892 the landlord was fined £1.00 for being drunk in charge of a horse and carriage and for assaulting a policeman.

Owned by Cooper's Brewery and renamed *The Haymarket*, it suffered extensive damage in World War Two and was rebuilt in 1965. The rear part, opened as *Limelight* in 1983, closed in 1988, and the site is now composed of retail outlets and apartments.

Hill Top Inn 118 Commercial Road

On the corner of Commercial Road and Sidford Street, on the approach to Four Posts Hill, it was built in 1901 on the site of an older pub of the same name. The original Cooper's Brewery pub had a beer licence prior to 1869 and the replacement pub was granted a full licence in March 1960.

Its licence was suspended in March 1972 with the building demolished in March 1973, and replaced by the Nelson Gate office block.

Horse and Groom 103 East Street

This was a well-known seaman's pub that had stood at the corner of East Street and Canal Walk since the early 1780s. It was known as the *Horse and Jockey* until about 1820 and is shown as fully licensed on the 1878 Drink Map. It was reputed to be one of the roughest and toughest in the town and fights were frequent, especially when the large transatlantic liners were docked in Southampton.

On 1 September 1959 an American sailor on the *USS Du Pont* was stabbed and murdered by a fellow seaman in front of the juke box in the lounge bar (left)

(See *Southampton's Murder Victims* by co-author Jim Brown).

(Hampshire Constabulary History Society)

Watney's Brewery allowed the licence to lapse in April 1973 and it was demolished soon after. A soft furnishing store now occupies the site.

The Inn Centre Portland Terrace

This Bass Charrington concrete pub opened in 1968 as the *Arundel Centre Inn* near the site of *Ye Olde Arundel Tower* pub at the bottom of Bargate Street, demolished in the mid-1960s when the newly built Inner Ring Road (Portland Terrace and Castle Way) cut it off.

The name changed to *Dog and Duck,* with the addition of a night club called *Barbarella's* in 1988.

Despite its Topless Go Go dancers it was not a success and, now called the *Inn Centre,* was demolished in the mid-1990s to make way for the below West Quay development.

(Bitterne Local History Society)

The John Barleycorn 17 Commercial Street

Dating back to the early 1870s and named after malt liquor and sometimes promoted to '*Sir*', it belonged to Barlow's Victoria Brewery before being owned by Brickwoods' Brewery.

Then a Whitbread's house, it closed for good in 1983 and was demolished soon after, with the Bitterne Health Centre now built on the site.

Jubilee Inn 7 Belvidere Road

On the corner of Belvidere and Victoria Roads and owned by Barlow's Victoria Brewery, it had a beer licence prior to 1869 and was granted a full licence on 8 March 1960. It later belonged to Brickwoods' Brewery and became a Whitbread's house in 1971.

It closed when its licence lapsed on 5 July 1974 and has since been demolished and replaced by Freeborn Garages Ltd, a Citroen dealer and garage.

London Arms 2 Victoria Road

The original pub on this site dates back to the early 1870s when Tom McLoriman was the licensee. Originally the property of Brickwoods' Brewery, it was destroyed in 1940 during the bombing of the Woolston area, when German bombers attacked the nearby Supermarine factory where Spitfires were assembled.

Rebuilt in the 1950s it became a Whitbread house in 1971, subsequently closed down and is now the Trafalgar Dental Practice.

Lord Louis West Marlands Road

Standing on the corner of West Marlands Road and Portland Terrace, this Strong's Romsey Brewery pub was opened in September 1960 by Lord Mountbatten, after whom it was named. It replaced the bombed *Brewery Bar* which had stood on the site.

It was taken over by the Whitbread Group in 1969 but closed in July 1987 and was demolished soon after. The site is now occupied by the Marlands shopping complex.

The Lord Palmerston 10/11 Palmerston Road

An Old Shirley Brewery pub called the *Star and Garter* in 1879 it was later owned by Cooper's Brewery. Palmerston Road was then called West Front. In June 1923 landlord Mr Avery was fined £40.00 for receiving two barrels of stolen beer. The name was changed to *Copperfield's* in 1983 with Phillip Barker as the licensee.

The older name was later restored but it closed sometime after and is now boarded up.

The Masons Wessex Lane

It occupies the site of an older Cooper's pub dating back to the 1830s when Tom Churcher was the licensee. Known as *The Mason's Arms* prior to 1984, it was the scene of much disorder from customers over the years and its reputation rapidly deteriorated.

The Masons closed down in late 1992 but re-opened a few months later. However, it eventually closed for good, was demolished and replaced by pleasant terraced housing.

Mason's Arms 45 St Mary Street

Another Mason's Arms, this time a Barlow's Victoria Brewery pub in the Chapel district. Standing on the corner of St Mary Street and St Mary's Buildings, it dates back to the 1860s. In March 1910 the landlord was fined 2/6d (12½ p) for selling drink to a police officer on duty and the following September 5/- (25p) for selling drink to a drunk person.

It later belonged to Brickwoods' Brewery, was taken into the Whitbread Group in 1971 and later owned by Gale's Horndean Brewery. It closed in 1994, and was occupied by squatters that November. This was eventually overcome and it is now private accommodation.

The Maybush Wimpson Lane

It opened as the *Maybush Hotel* in March 1956 with its first landlord, Tony Mulvarney. It had a name change to *Top's* at the end of 1984 after extensive alterations and refurbishment, catering mainly for the younger age group specialising in loud music.

However, it had closed by January 1992 and was boarded up until that summer when it re-opened as the *Maybush,* still catering for the younger age group. By 2013 it had once again closed and during 2014 demolished with new housing under construction on the site.

The Merry Oak 104 Spring Road

Standing on the corner of Spring and Deacon Roads, it was built in 1931 for Brickwoods' Brewery and in 1971 it became a Whitbread house. A very successful pub for many years, it slowly deteriorated and closed around 2011/12.

It was later converted into a Veterinary Surgery called Vets4Pets who aroused some controversy over its parking arrangements. Its car park was adjacent to a Tesco Convenience Store, whose customers found it useful to park there. Vet4Pets brought in a car clamping firm who were merciless in clamping almost before drivers had left the car park.

Morning Star 37 Terminus Terrace

Standing on the corner of Terminus Terrace and Marsh Lane, this Aldridge's Bedford Brewery pub dates back to the 1850s when William Philpot was the landlord and the 1878 Drink Map shows it was then fully licensed. It closed in 1933 and was used as apartments.

It is believed that the building was destroyed during World War Two and the site is now derelict, but with the massive Dukes Keep office block adjacent and in the background.

Mount Hotel 67 Bevois Valley Road

Standing on the corner of Bevois Valley Road and Ancasta Road, it dates back to the 1850s when George Hellier was the licensee. It is shown as a beer house on the 1878 Drink Map.

It closed, as a Watney's house, in 1958 and was used as a scrap merchant's office for some time, before being demolished and the present apartment block built on the site.

(Genevieve Bailey)

The Nag's Head 42 High Street

The original *Nag's Head* received its name around 1740 when George Burcy ran it. Mr Burcy came from the nearby *Red Lion* (dating from before 1552) at 55 High Street. This is believed to have also been called the *Nag's Head* and that he brought the name with him when he took over No. 42.

A closer view of the self-explanatory decoration at the top of the building.

(Genevieve Bailey)

It was destroyed in the blitz of World War Two and replaced by this temporary building, now a Watney's house, on the same site.

In November 1957 the temporary shack was replaced by a new structure, still called the *Nag's Head*, on the corner of High Street and Bernard Street.

It was renamed *Fiddlers* in 1991 but subsequently closed and is now called *Zen*, a contemporary Japanese bar and restaurant.

New Farm House 22 Mount Pleasant Road

Standing on the corner of Mount Pleasant and Derby Roads, it dates back to the early 1870s when Silas Lush was the landlord and is shown as fully licensed on the 1878 Drink Map. It was originally owned by Aldridge's Bedford Brewery but later belonged to Brickwoods' Brewery until taken over by the Whitbread Group in 1971.

It narrowly escaped destruction on the night of 10 April 1941 when the lower part of Derby and Northumberland Roads were destroyed by a single landmine.

The pub was named to compare with the *Old Farm House* at No. 39, opened directly opposite as a beer house in 1843. It ceased trading on 30 August 1980 and is now a private residence.

New Forest Stag 32 Amoy Street

Standing on the corner of Amoy and Henry Streets, it had a beer licence prior to 1869 and is said to have been built on the site of an old house where George IV (1762-1830) stopped for refreshment when hunting in the area. He is said to have liked the home-made beer so much that he granted the occupant an immediate licence. In view of the date of his death this story is possibly inaccurate.

The property of the Winchester Brewery it was granted a full licence in July 1960 but this was suspended in July 1972 and the building, then a Marston's house, demolished shortly afterwards. A car park was later built on the site.

The Newlands 597 Portswood Road

On the corner of Portswood and Kitchener Roads, it was known as the *New Inn* in 1803 when David Churcher was the landlord. The 1878 Drink Map shows it was then fully licensed. The name changed to *Newlands Hotel* in the 1920s, probably when the present building was erected, and it became the *Prince Regent* in May 1983. Because customers disliked the new name, it reverted to just the *Newlands* in 1986.

Although it had several landlords, its reputation deteriorated and it was forced to close in the summer of 1991. It became semi-derelict and the victim of an arson attack in January 1992, forcing its demolition, with new apartments built on the site.

The Newtown Inn 8 9 St Mary's Road

Standing on the corner of St Mary's and Onslow Roads, it dates back to the early 1860s when J. Stone was the landlord and its address was 1 Newtown Terrace. Belonging to Panton's Wareham Brewery in 1881, it was bought by Scrase's Star Brewery in 1892, later owned by Strong's Romsey Brewery and finally the Whitebread Group in 1969.

It closed for refurbishment in 1984, re-opening as the *Bitter End*, but after a change of ownership in 1993 it changed again, this time to the *Oliver Goldsmith's*. It is now the *Best One* convenience store.

North Star 92 St Mary Street

Alfred Ireland established a small brewery and beer shop in these premises in 1851 and named it after *HMS North Star* on which he once served. It was the property of Welsh'e Hyde Abbey Brewery, later Cooper's Brewery and finally a Watney's house. It closed down after a serious fire in 1989 but re-opened in 1991.

It subsequently closed down when during 2000/2004 the previous shops were demolished and the area drastically redeveloped with modern housing.

Northumberland Arms 55/57 Northumberland Road

On the corner of Northumberland and St Albans Roads, this Welsh's Hyde Abbey Brewery pub dates back to the early 1880s when Philp Pomeroy was the landlord. In 1920 the landlord F. Hopkins was fined £5.00 for permitting gambling on the premises and in 1929 it was taken over by Cooper's Brewery. It changed to a Watney's house for many years but in early 1988 it was closed because of drug use.

After a major fire in 1990 it closed completely and was occupied by squatters for a couple of years before it finally burned to the ground in April 1994. Built in 2009 and opened in 2010, the site became a Muslim Cultural Centre and a Muslim private primary school called Fitrah SIPS (Southampton Islamic Primary School).

Number One Inn 76 Mount Pleasant Road

When Barlow's Victoria Brewery leased the premises in early 1900s its address was 1, Spring Place, Mount Pleasant – thus called *Number One Inn.* Only a licenced beer house prior to 1869, it was granted a full licence in 1961 and became tied to Brickwoods' Brewery. The licence was suspended on 23 March 1969 and the empty building gutted by an arson attack that May. It was demolished shortly afterwards, with the site derelict for some considerable time.

The site, directly adjacent to Mount Pleasant Junior School, is now occupied by a very pleasant 'Mount Pleasant Open Space' with trees, grass and seating.

Old Arundel Tower Hotel 22 Bargate Street

Originally called the *Plumber's Arms* in 1853, when Richard Bow, a plumber, painter and glazier was landlord, the name changed to *The Old Tower Inn* in the mid-1870s. It was a fully licensed house on the 1878 Drink Map, associated with Lankaster's Albion Brewery. Taken over by Eldridge Pope's Dorchester Brewery in 1885, it was demolished in 1899 and replaced with the above structure, with the name *Old Arundel Tower Hotel*. It was badly damaged during the World War Two blitz and closed from November 1940 to June 1941 after repair.

It was finally demolished in the mid-1960s when the Inner Ring Road was built.

Old Gates Hotel Blechynden Street

Owned by Aldridge's Bedford Brewery, it was known as the *Southampton West Hotel* until the middle 1930s, so called because of its proximity to the Southampton West Railway Station. In July 1919 the landlord, Mr Alcock, was fined £2.00 for selling gin over the maximum permitted price.

It was destroyed during the blitzkrieg bombing of World War Two in 1942 and in 1970 the site was acquired for development by Southampton City Council.

Old Shirley Brewery Tap Romsey Road

Built in the early 19th century as a tap bar for the nearby Old Shirley Brewery, which was then owned by brewers Barlow and Clode, it was later taken over by the Winchester Brewery. It was refused a licence in 1913 and was forced to close. As a result the brewery received £1,114 12s in compensation.

The site is now occupied by a Peugeot car dealership.

Old Thatched House 219 Romsey Road

At the junction of Romsey Road and Winchester Road, this was the only thatched pub left in Southampton. Several hundred years old, it was a beer house in the 1890s owned by Alice Saunders and later the property of the People's Refreshment House Association. It was taken over by Bass Charington in early 1974, closed for a major refurbishment early in 1984 and reopened that July.

It eventually closed and has now been transformed into the St James Chiropractic Clinic, offering a wide range of chiropractic massage and Pilates treatment.

Oliver Cromwell Millbrook Road

Said to be over 400 years old it received its name from a story that Oliver Cromwell stayed there overnight on his way to Southampton during the Civil War. Once owned by the Winchester Brewery it later belonged to the London based Charrington's Anchor Brewery.

Its licence was suspended on 22 May 1967 and it was demolished shortly afterwards. The west-bound carriageway of Millbrook Road now crosses the site.

The Oriental 29 Queens Terrace

A Grade II listed building and shown on the 1870 town map, it was known as *Kelway's Hotel* in the 1880s and then *Kelway's Oriental Hotel* until February 1906 when it received its present name. A Berni Inn from 1964 it became a bar/restaurant in 1987 but closed after a few months. It belonged to various brewers until becoming the property of the Whitbread Group in 1971. It reopened December 1988 as a 'pub/diner', continuing as such until it eventually closed down in the late 1990s and was converted into flats.

Taking a comparative photo was difficult because Queens Terrace is currently undergoing extensive redevelopment as part of the new road network catering for the cruise liner trade.

Oxford Hotel 126 St Mary's Road

Standing on the corner of St Mary's and Brintons Roads, it was shown as a fully licensed house on the 1878 Drink Map. Owned by Barlow's Victoria Brewery its address was then 97 St Mary's Road and the landlord W. Cull. It later became the property of Brickwoods' Brewery and a Whitbread's house in 1971.

It eventually ceased to trade and was converted into flats.

Park Hotel 90 Shirley Road

Standing on the corner of Shirley and Sir George's Roads, it was owned by Eldridge Pope's Dorchester Brewery in 1878 and was then known as the *Park House Inn*. It was one of the few to then have a billiard room, but this fell into disuse and it became an entertainment room with a Hammond organ.

It later became a pool hall, but eventually closed down in 2013 and is now awaiting either conversion or development.

Pembroke Hotel 6 Pembroke Square

At the end of a tiny cul-de-sac alongside and to the east of The Bargate, it stood on the site of a medieval tavern called the *New Inn*. Renamed *Lion Inn* in the 16th century it became the *Red Lion* in the 18th century and the square called *Red Lion Square*. It had various names after that, such as *Golden Anchor* in 1852 and *Bargate Tavern* in 1861, before becoming the *Pembroke Hotel* in the late 19th century.

Both the square and the pub were demolished when the eastern side of the Bargate was developed in the 1930s.

(*Bitterne Local History Society*)

Percy Arms 18 Commercial Street

The property of Crowley's Alton Brewery and formerly called the *Commercial Inn*, it opened at the end of the 19th century and became a Watney's pub in 1947.

It closed in 2010 and in 2011 became the *pharmacy DIRECT*, nostalgically retaining the old pub name on the walls.

Portland Arms 69 Above Bar Street

(*Bitterne Local History Society*)

Standing on the corner of Above Bar Street and Regent Street, this pub was renowned as the smallest pub in Southampton. It dated back to the 1830s when Mrs Taplin was the landlady and the 1878 Drink Map shows it to have been a beer house. Its address at that time was the strange 59½ Above Bar Street and it was owned by Cooper's Brewery and later a Watney's house.

It was very popular with reporters from the nearby Southampton Daily Echo and seamen visiting the port, who knew it as *The Snug* because of its small interior. It was granted a full licence on 8 July 1960 but closed for good on 31 August 1971 with Ron Snow as its last licensee. The building then became an employment agency, later a boutique before being finally demolished in November 1993.

The photo showing the adjacent Odeon Cinema, opened as the Regal Cinema in 1934, shows the *Portland Arms* in perspective. The entire block has since been fully developed.

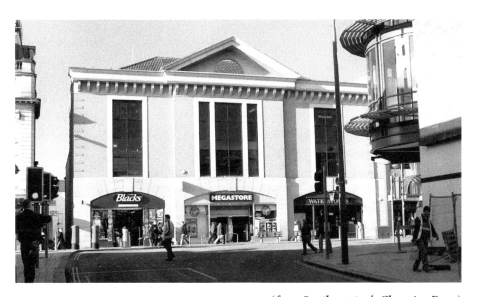

(*from Southampton's Changing Faces*)

(Cobwebs Collection – Peter Boyd-Smith)

Pound Tree Inn 7 Pound Tree Road

Standing on the corner of Pound Tree and Sussex Roads, this Winchester Brewery pub had a licence prior to 1869. It was later owned by Marston's Brewery but was completely destroyed during the World War Two blitzkrieg. The licence, however, remained suspended until 1957 when it was transferred to the *Freemantle Arms* in Albany Road.

Modern *Ruby's Nails & Beauty* salon and vacant offices now occupy the site.

Princess Royal 10 Mount Street

Standing on the corner of Mount Street and Cross Street, it dates back to the 1850s when the landlord, Ben Vivian, who was also a grocer, ran the premises. Owned by Barlow's Victoria Brewery, it was refused a licence in 1910 and the brewery received £1,112.00 in compensation. The whole area has since been developed and modern flats now stand on the site.

Queen's Hotel 173 Albert Road

One of six consecutive pubs now vanished from Albert Road, it dates back to the 1850s when Israel Eden was the landlord, and the 1878 Drink Map shows it was fully licensed. In January1917 and again in December 1917 the landlord and landlady were each fined for selling drinks outside permitted hours. Demolished in the late 2000s as a Bass Charrington house, the site has been an unfinished apartment construction for the past few years.

Queensland Tavern 78 Clovelly Road

Standing on the corner of Clovelly and Exmoor Roads, it first opened in the 1890s as the *Queensland Hotel*. The property of Barlow's Victoria Brewery it was later owned by Brickwoods' Brewery and by 1971 became a Whitbread house.

It has now suffered the fate of many similar public houses and has been converted into a private dwelling.

*(**Henry Brain Collection – Maureen Webber**)*

The Railway Hotel 102 Osborne Road

Standing on the corner of Osborne and St Denys Roads, the original building was the old Portswood Railway Station but was demolished when the Portsmouth line was opened in the 1860s. The above premises were built shortly after and the 1878 Drink Map shows it was fully licensed. In July 1892 the landlord was fined £2.00 for selling adulterated whisky.

Originally owned by Cooper's Brewery, later Watney's, it was demolished in 1986 to make way for the Portswood/Swaythling 'Thomas Lewis Way' dual carriageway bypass.

Railway Tavern 1 Albert Road

Standing on the corner of Albert Road and Elm Street and owned by Cooper's Brewery, it dates back to the 1840s when Charles Robinson, also a blacksmith, was the licensee. The 1878 Drink Map shows it as fully licensed.

Yet another one of the now vanished public houses in Albert Road, it was so badly bomb damaged in World War Two that it had to be demolished. The site is still vacant.

Railway Tavern 12 Blechynden Terrace

It dated back to the 1830s when a Mr Hill was the landlord and was shown as an Eldridge Pope's Dorchester Brewery beer house on the 1878 Drink Map. It became the *West Station Tavern* between 1900 and 1930 but then reverted back to *Railway Tavern*. It was destroyed on the night of 22 June 1940 during the Second World War blitzkrieg. The landlord, Arthur Collett and his wife were both killed.

The licence was suspended on 21 October 1942 and in 1968 the site was acquired by the local authority by compulsory purchase for development.

Red Lion 32 Cannon Street

It was owned by the Winchester Brewery in the early 1900s and was privately owned from 1922. It closed in the 1930s and was an off-licence for many years, then a radio shop supplying a Rediffusion service (as advertised above, the premises shown boarded up), that supplied a cable radio service to houses. It was demolished when the area was developed in the 1960s.

All traces have now vanished and the area has a pleasant appearance.

The Richard Andrews 5 New Road

Shown as a beer house on the 1878 Drink Map, it had a wine and beer licence prior to 1869. Owned by Gibb Mew's Salisbury Brewery, it was named after Richard Andrews, a local coach maker and leader of the Liberal Party.

It was demolished in 1957 in order to build what was then the Southampton Institute, since transformed into the Solent University.

The Rising Sun 73 Botany Bay Road

Dating back to the mid-1800s, with Harry Riddle as landlord, it was the property of the Winchester Brewery until it later became a Marston's house. The address was shown as 44 Botany Bay Road until the 1960s. It had closed by the end of 1990 and re-opened as a free house called the *Water Garden* by the end of 1994. However, the sign of the *Rising Sun* remained on the wall.

All traces of the former pub have gone and it is now a nicely decorated private residence, currently up for rent.

Robert Burns 163/165 Albert Road

One of a line of six consecutive pubs along Albert Road, it dates back to the 1870s and shown as a beer house on the 1878 Drink Map. Owned by Cooper's Brewery until the 1940s, when it became a Watney's house, it was taken over by Bass Charrington on 15 November 1978.

It closed for good in 1980 and it was later demolished. An uncompleted building currently occupies the site and further development has been delayed for some years.

Robert Burns 9 South Front

Standing on the corner of South Front and Middle Street, it dated back to the 1860s when William Hickman was the landlord. The 1878 Drink Map shows it was a beer house and it was first owned by the Eldridge Pope's Dorchester Brewery in January 1893.

Middle Street is now Cossack Green and the former pub has been replaced by modern apartments. The entire area has been developed and the former South Front also consists of modern housing.

Rose, Shamrock & Thistle 13 Royal Crescent Road

On the corner of Royal Crescent Road and Lower Bridge Road, the former Barlow's Victoria Brewery pub dates back to the 1870s and is shown as fully licensed on the 1878 Drink Map. In December 1918 landlord Onigin Hoffman was fined £25.00 for selling beer over the maximum permitted price.

Its licence was suspended on 29 November 1968 and the building demolished shortly after. This was part and parcel of the wholesale development of the area in preparation for the construction of the Itchen Bridge.

Royal Albert 123 Albert Road

A Grade II listed building standing on the corner of Albert and Lower Bridge Roads, named in honour of Queen Victoria's husband, it dates back to the early 1850s when the landlord was James Stratton. Owned by Scrase's Star Brewery, the 1878 Drink Map shows it as fully licensed. Later owned by Strong's Romsey Brewery it became a Whitbread pub in 1969.

It was scheduled for demolition as part of the development of the area in 1975, but because it is listed was saved. It closed in the late 1990s and was converted into flats.

Royal Albert 23 Marlborough Road

This originally Aldridge's Bedford Brewery pub was a beer house in 1859 when James White was the landlord and was granted a full licence in March 1960. Small, and located in a terrace of houses in what used to be called Oxford Street, it later became the property of Brickwoods' Brewery.

It closed in 1970 and was later demolished. The site is now a car park.

Royal Mail Millbrook Road

A former coaching inn, said to be over 300 years old, it stood on the bank of Tanner's Brook and belonged to Strong's Romsey Brewery. In October 1918 landlord Charles Butt was fined £2.00 for selling drink outside permitted hours.

Its licence was suspended on 22 March 1967 and it was demolished soon after for the widening of Millbrook Road. The west-bound carriageway now runs over the site.

Royal Oak Hazel Road

The original *Royal Oak* stood near this site, on the banks of the River Itchen, and dated back several hundred years, serving those travelling across the river by the Itchen Ferrymen. It was rebuilt and relocated at the end of the 19th century, a feature of what was then called Itchen Ferry Village.

The *Royal Oak* was almost destroyed in a 1942 enemy air raid of World War Two, when the nearby Supermarine Works, where Spitfires were built, was destroyed. However, a small pillar (inset above) of this old pub still remains. (It can also be just seen to the right of the car parked on the pavement)

Royal Oak Wimpson Lane

The original *Royal Oak* was a pub located in what was then the heart of the countryside, well outside the boundary of Southampton. It had been there for several hundred years, catering for east/west bound travellers. However, following the extensive redevelopment of the area in 1965, it was demolished. A new public house, of the same name, was built behind the site of the old building at a cost of £29,000 and opened on 20 October 1965. It was a Strong's Romsey Brewery house, later part of the Whitbread Group.

The pub closed in 2010 and was replaced by a One-Stop convenience store and a fish and chip shop.

Royal Sovereign 25 Millbank Street

Standing on the corner of Millbank Street and what remains of Kent Street, it dates back to the 1850s when George Newman was the landlord. The 1878 Drink Map shows it as a beer house. Owned by Cooper's Brewery, later Watney's, it became the property of Gibbs Mew's Salisbury Brewery in 1989.

It closed early in 1994, became derelict and occupied by squatters for some time. They ran a shebeen from the premises, until it was eventually demolished with council housing built on the site.

The Russell Tavern 6 Russell Street

Standing on the corner of Russell and King Streets, it dates back to the early 1850s when Mr W. Kent was the landlord. The property of the Winchester Brewery it was known as the *Ship Inn* until the early 1890s, when it received its present name.

It was later bought by Marston's Brewery and its licence suspended 13 February 1956 and by 1960 the area had been fully developed with housing.

Sailor's Home 97 Bevois Street

Standing on the corner of Bevois and Grove Streets, it had a beer licence prior to 1869 and the 1878 Drink Map shows it as a beer house. This striking looking pub, with its Tudor appearance, was the property of Barlow's Victoria Brewery until it later became a Brickwoods' house.

It closed in 1962 and was demolished soon after, with a pleasant floral garden and council housing developed on the site.

Sailor's Return 309 Millbrook Road

On the corner of Millbrook Road and Waterhouse Lane, this Cooper's Brewery pub dates back to the 1860s when Jacob Bush was the landlord. It became part of Watney, Coombe and Reid by 1945, had a major refurbishment, at a cost of £50,000, and reopened in December 1983.

Following the widening of Millbrook Road in the late 1960s and the development of the dual carriageway, it became isolated from the main traffic and eventually closed by 2001. It was demolished and the St John Ambulance Millbrook Headquarters built on the site, which also houses their Commercial Patient Transport Service.

Sawyer's Arms 4 Nelson Road

Dating back to the 1850s, when the landlord was H. Ashby, this Welsh's Lion Brewery pub was later owned by Mew Langton's Newport Brewery. In April 1917 the landlord, Mr Dunsford, was fined 10/- (50p) for being drunk in charge of a horse and carriage.

It was destroyed by a bomb in World War Two and the site later occupied by pre-fabricated houses. These have since been replaced by blocks of apartments.

Scullards 2 Pound Tree Road

There were three pubs bearing the name *Scullards,* all on different sites in Above Bar, before this one in Pound Tree Road. All originated from the 19th century hotel founded by Charles Scullard. This site was originally occupied by the *Park Inn* in the late 1950s, spared in wartime bombing but, owned by Watney, Coombe and Reid, demolished when the area was developed.

The *Park Inn* closed for refurbishment in May 1986 and re-opened later that year under the familiar name of *Scullards.* It closed in October 1990 and is now a betting shop.

The Seaweed Inn Weston Lane

Named after the famed old "seaweed hut" fisherman's store that stood on the shoreline at the bottom of Weston Lane, with its roof covered in seaweed and sides with large planks, it opened on 15 March 1967. It was a free house but later taken over by Courage's Brewery.

It had closed by August 2003, when the City Council approved the renaming of the road as The Chandlers, whilst Foreman Homes were in the process of building 56 flats on the site formerly occupied by the *Seaweed Hut*.

Ship Tavern 5 Canute Road

Dating back to the 1850s when Tom McLoriman was the landlord, it shows as a beer house on the 1878 Drink Map and was owned by Aldridge's Bedford Brewery. The licence was suspended in 1933 and the brewery received £2,025. 15s compensation when the pub closed. It was badly damaged by bombing in 1940, but became a café. The words *London and Dublin Stout House* can still just be seen on the upper wall.

The premises became a 'Gurkha Kitchen' restaurant in the late 2000s but it has now closed and the premises are boarded up. The words on the wall can still be seen today, although very faint.

Shipwright's Arms 4 Elm Terrace

This Barlow's Victoria Brewery pub was known as the _Joiner's Arms_ in 1871, very probably because George Joyner was the landlord, but was refused a licence in 1924 and closed. The brewery then received the considerable sum of £2,639 17s 6d in compensation.

The site is now occupied by Southampton City Council Supply Services.

The Smugglers 114 Bernard Street

Standing on the corner of Bernard Street and Threefield Lane, this Cooper's Brewery pub dates back to the late 1850s when Henry Adams was the landlord. It was known as the *Richmond Inn* and *Richmond Tavern* until the early 1980s. It was recorded as being at 37 Bridge Road, before the road changed to become Bernard Street.

Later a Watney's House, it was then owned by Belhaven, a Scottish brewery. Still known as *Smugglers* in 2007, it later closed and replaced by a block of apartments.

Spa Tavern 16 Spa Road

Dating back to the 1850s when William Hyde was the landlord, it was owned by Aldridge's Bedford Brewery, then Cooper's Brewery. Several landlords and landladies were fined in 1903, 1908 and 1912 for allowing drunkenness on the premises, and in 1924 it was refused a licence. The brewers appealed and it was renewed the following year.

In an alley running alongside the former Echo office block, they were all demolished by 1997 as part of the creation of the West Quay Shopping Centre.

The Spring Spring Road

Standing on the corner of Spring and Rosoman Roads, it dates back to 1900 when the licence from the *George Inn* in Hazel Road was transferred. Owned by Cooper's Brewery, then Watney's, it became a free house, but in the early 1980s the landlord tried to change its image and changed its name to the *Muddled Man*. This was unpopular with locals so it reverted back to *The Spring* in 1984.

Changing the name back did not succeed altogether so trade gradually died off and it was eventually demolished and modern apartments built on the site.

St Leonard's 130 Northam Road

Standing on the corner of Northam Road and Kent Street, it dates back to 1855 when James Blake was the landlord. The 1878 Drink Map shows it as a beer house when it was owned by Cooper's Brewery, but it was a Watney's house when it was demolished in the 1960s.

It was then replaced by a pub called the *Telstar,* the name of an early communications satellite. Name change again in 1989 to *Pitcher's,* after it was taken over by Belhaven Scottish Brewery, it changed back to *St Leonard's* towards the end of 1992, but later closed altogether, was demolished and a housing development built on the site.

St Mary's Hotel 65 East Street

The original pub on this site, at the very bottom of East Street, had its own brewery when Mrs Higgins was the landlady in 1843, but it was demolished and rebuilt in the 'Tudor' style in the 1930s. The property of Strong's Romsey Brewery for many years it became part of the Whitbread Group in 1969. The licence was suspended on 23 June 1972 and it was demolished shortly afterwards.

The former East Street Shopping Centre was then built on the site but in 2014 this, in turn, was also demolished (after the above photo was taken) and is awaiting the construction of a large Morrisons Shopping Centre on the site.

Standard of Freedom 51 Belvidere Terrace

On the corner of Belvidere Terrace and Peel Street, it was the property of Aldridge's Bedford Brewery. It dates back to the 1850s when Tom Tundle was the landlord and is shown as a fully licensed house in the 1878 Drink Map. In February 1917 the landlord, Alfred McDonald, was fined £5 for selling drink outside permitted hours.

It was destroyed in 1941 during the blitzkrieg and replaced by an industrial site.

Star & Garter 50 Waterloo Road

Standing on the corner of Waterloo Road and Park Road, this Cooper's Brewery pub dates back to the 1860s when Robert Culley was the landlord. It was then called the *Star Hotel* but changed to *Star & Garter* in 1899. It became a Watney's house but had closed by 2006.

It was demolished in the summer of 2007 and replaced by a block of apartments.

Star Inn 132 Avenue Road

Standing on the corner of Avenue and Spear Roads, it dates back to the early 1870s when grocer Eli Rose was the landlord. The property of Aldridge's Bedford Brewery, it is shown as a beer house on the 1878 Drink Map. It later belonged to Brickwoods' Brewery and the property of the Whitbread Group in 1971.

Now closed and converted to private accommodation

Station Hotel Blechynden Terrace

Originally the *West Station Hotel* was shown on this site (on the far left of the photo) on the 1870 town map. It changed to *Station Hotel* in March 1935 and was the property of Cooper's Brewery. It was destroyed during World War Two and the above Watney's temporary single-storeyed building erected on the site at a cost of £300.00.

It was acquired by the local authority under a compulsory purchase order on 20 June 1972 and later demolished. The area has since been developed beyond recognition

Stoneham Arms 109 Bassett Green Road

This fine Tudor style pub opened in 1933, obtaining its licence by transfer when the *George Inn* in Above Bar closed. The property of Strong's Romsey Brewery, it became a Whitbread house in 1969.

It closed on 1 August 2013 and is now a large Co-operative Supermarket serving the area, open from 7.00am to 10.00pm seven days a week (8.00am on Sundays).

Sun Hotel 84 High Street

On the corner of High Street and the Town Quay, this Cooper's Brewery fully licensed pub dates back to 1783 when John Fowler was the landlord. It was destroyed during the bombing of World War Two and replaced by a "temporary" wood shack that lasted for nearly 50 years.

Local folklore says it was built by thirsty Canadians just prior to D-Day in June 1944, but this is clearly a myth.

The foundations of the old pub could be seen under the wooden shack, which closed in June 1990, demolished in 1994 and now replaced by flats and houses.

Sun Inn Weston Lane

Dating back to the 1830s when John Cole was the landlord, this Scrase's Star Brewery building was a quiet little country pub in a small winding lane. It later became the property of Strong's Romsey Brewery but was taken over by the Whitbread Group in 1969.

Now on the corner of the newly created Camley Close, the pub closed, was demolished and replaced by the Weston Lane Surgery, Pharmacy, Dental and Hearing services.

(Keith Bullmore)

Surrey Hotel 57 Orchard Place

Originally in Orchard Place, on the corner of Queens Terrace, these Barlow's Victoria Brewery premises dated back to the 1840s. In February 1909 landlord Christopher Thomas Bullmore was fined 5/- (25p) for selling beer to a drunken person. At a later period the premises were extended to have a much grander frontage in Queens Terrace, with the proprietor proudly standing in the doorway. It was demolished and rebuilt in the 1950s.

(*Keith Bullmore*)

Christopher Thomas Bullmore and his first wife Fanny stand behind the bar, ready to serve their customers.

These behind the bar of the *Surrey Hotel* are unknown but believed to be possibly the landlord with his family and staff after Christopher Thomas Bullmore retired in the 1930s.

The pub was completely rebuilt and the name changed to *Rum Runners* in the early 1980s but it closed for good, as a Whitbread's house, in the summer of 1988.

Not long after, once again demolished, but this time replaced by a modern office block.

Sussex Hotel 86/88 Above Bar Street

Standing on the corner of Above Bar Street and Sussex Place, this Barlow's Victoria Brewery pub was originally known as the *Sussex Wine & Spirit Vaults* before changing to the *Sussex Hotel*. It survived the extensive bombing throughout the area during World War Two, only to be demolished in the early 1960s. A new Brickwoods' Brewery building, with the same name, was built on the site.

The new building, part of a row of shops running from Palmerston Park to the corner of Pound Tree Road, was not successful, probably because it only had one huge bar that had to be entered via a long dark passageway. It closed in 1967 and was replaced by several shops that have since changed owners several times.

The Swan Redbridge Road

The original pub was adjacent to the old Millbrook Pond alongside the main Southampton to Bournemouth Millbrook Road. The landlord was named in the Southampton 1851 street directory as C. M'Kay, beer retailer and draper. It was demolished in the late 1960s to make room for the new Millbrook Flyover.

A new pub, the *Fighting Cocks* was built at a cost of £40,000, not far from the site and opened on 26 November 1968. It became the property of the Whitbread Group in 1971 and reverted to *The Swan* in 1988. It later closed and became a Kentucky Fried Chicken restaurant.

The Target Butts Road

Built around the 1930s and standing on the corner of Butts and Bursledon Roads, it was a large family pub the property of Brickwoods' Brewery. The landlord was Edward Lionel McLachlan from before 1940 to at least 1951.

Its name, *The Target,* as well as the nearby pub, *The Bulls Eye,* and local roads such as Butts Road, Dragoon Close and Shooters Hill Close, all relate to the fact that Sholing Common was home to a Volunteer Rifle Range in the 1880s.

It closed in the early 2000s and was demolished with a large block of pleasant apartments built on the site.

The Three Swans 84 Albert Road

Leased to Eldridge Pope's Dorchester Brewery since June 1866 and shown on the 1870 town map as at 55 Andersons Terrace, it had its own brewery. It temporarily closed in April 1941 so that bomb damage could be repaired, but was acquired under a compulsory purchase order on 19 August 1967 in order to build the Itchen Bridge.

It was then demolished during the bridge construction and now lies under it around this point.

Tudors 97 Coxford Road

The original Strong's Brewery pub on this site, dating back to the 1870s, was called the *Brickmaker's Arms*, after the many brickfields in the area. It became fully licensed in 1938, probably when the present building was constructed on the site. The 1951 street directory shows Stanley Woodhouse as licensee of the *Brickmaker's Arms*.

It became the property of the Whitbread Group in 1969, changed its name to *Tudors* in September 1986, following a major refurbishment, but closed in the mid-1990s. It was finally demolished in 2001 and replaced by the above large block of flats.

PUBLIC BAR
PRICE LIST

	Maximum Price per Small Bottle
WATNEYS PALE & BROWN ALE	1/2
MANNS	1/4
RED BARREL EXPORT/P.A.	1/6½
CREAM LABEL STOUT	1/0½
STINGO	2/6½
BASS BLUE TRIANGLE	1/9
WORTHINGTON GREEN SHIELD	1/9
DOUBLE DIAMOND	1/9
SKOL LAGER & CARLINGS LAGER	1/9½

	per Nip
RED BARREL EXPORT P.A.	1/2½
EXPORT GOLD PALE BARLEY WINE	1/9½
STINGO BARLEY WINE	1/10½

	per Pint
MILD ALE	1/7
ALTON BITTER	1/10
SPECIAL BITTER	2/1
WATNEYS RED BARREL	2/3
WATNEYS SPECIAL MILD	1/8
STAR LIGHT	1/10

WATNEY COMBE REID (ALTON) LIMITED

(Genevieve Bailey)

The Victory Nelson Gate

Standing opposite the north entrance to Southampton's main railway station, it was a Hall and Woodhouse pub erected in the 1970s close to the site of the former old *Coachmaker's Arms* in what used to be Sidford Street.

It closed in 2006 and the bulk of the building is currently being advertised for shops and offices rental. The right hand section has become a Costa Coffee shop.

White Hart Hotel 49 Shirley High Street

This Winchester Breery pub, shown on the near right of the picture, was in Shirley High Street in the 1850s, when Francis Collins was the landlord. It later became a Marston's house and after its licence expired on 9 February 1982 it was demolished.

The former pub site now houses the premises of the Superdrug chemist chain.

White Star 32 Chapel Road

This Aldridge's Bedford Brewery pub that dates back to the early 1860s when J. Goding was the licensee, stood on the corner of Chapel Road and Granville Road. The 1878 Drink Map shows it was fully licensed. It was known as the *Blue Anchor Inn* until 12 February 1907.

It finally closed in the 1930s and the building had a number of other occupants until it was demolished in the 1960s when the area was developed. The site is now occupied by industrial units.

Wig & Pen 7 Spa Road

Dating back to the 1850s when Jacob Bush was the landlord, this Scrase's Star Brewery pub is shown as a beer house on the 1878 Drink Map. It received a full licence on 5 April 1959. Originally known as *The Running Horse* and owned by the Whitbread Group in 1969, it was seriously damaged by fire in March 1986 and after refurbishment re-opened as the *Wig & Pen*.

It was demolished by 1997 as part of the creation of the West Quay Shopping Centre and the site is buried underneath buildings behind the Bargate Medical Centre at 1 Spa Road.

The Windsor 23 Windsor Terrace

There has been an Inn or Hotel on this site since 1840, when James Weeks was the landlord. It became the property of Winchester Brewery in 1894 and was then surrounded by beautiful gardens as though in the countryside. Adjacent to the former bus station, it became a Marston's house but the entire street was demolished in 1987 for development.

Both the bus station and the pub site are now covered by the Marlands Shopping Complex.

The Winning Post 82/84 Pear Tree Avenue

Standing on the corner of Pear Tree Avenue and Merridale Road, Cooper's Brewery tried to obtain a licence in 1932, when the Merry Oak garden estate was being developed, but local opposition delayed the application until it was granted on the fourth attempt in 1937. The building was then constructed and opened in 1939. It then served a newly built 51 acre estate that had been compulsorily purchased for the surprising sum of just £32,567, with new roads named after ornamental trees.

The pub had closed by around 2008 but instead of being demolished for housing, as so often happens, it had a change of use and is now a One Stop convenience store.

(Cobwebs Collection – Peter Boyd-Smith)

The Wonder Inn 182 Northam Road

Standing on the corner of Northam Road and York Street, in what used to be called Paradise Row, it was named after an old Channel Island paddle steamer. It was a private house until it opened as a pub in 1855 with William Galton as landlord. A beer house on the 1878 Drink Map, it was original a Cooper's Brewery property but was later a Watney's house.

It closed in 1958 and was subsequently demolished to make was for the construction of a row of shops and tower blocks at the rear.

The Woodman Lordswood Road

Located on the corner of Lordswood and Coxford Roads, it was built for Strong's Romsey Brewery in the early 1950s and opened on 19 January 1954. The first licensee was Fred Weston, a former Detective Constable stationed at Shirley Police Station and a colleague of co-author Jim Brown, who later also served as a Detective Constable at Shirley.

It closed in 2011 and was converted into a Tesco Express convenience store.

WALTER J. HITCH,

Stag Brewery,

HIGHFIELD,

SOUTHAMPTON,

Supplies the following ALES, STOUT, & PORTER
of excellent quality, and in splendid condition.

PRICE LIST.

			Per 9 Galls.		
Mild Ale Extra Strength	XXX	15/0	13/6	12/0
Do. do. - -	XX	9/0		
Do. do. - -	X	7/6		
India Pale Ale	IPA	15/0	13/6	12/0
HITCH'S SPECIALTY Strongly recommended for Family Use	HS	10/6		
Bitter Ale - - -	AK	9/0		
Double Stout - -	SS	15/0	13/6	
Single do. - -	S	12/0		
Porter - - -	P	9/0		

ORDERS BY POST PROMPTLY EXECUTED.

Supplied also in 4½, 6, 18, and 36 Gallon Casks.

Daily Delivery in Southampton and Neighbourhood.

ND - #0314 - 270225 - C0 - 234/156/11 - PB - 9781780914510 - Gloss Lamination